S0-BYV-576

Livonia Public Library
ALFRED NOBLE BRANCH
32901 PLYMOUTH ROAD
Livonia, Michigan 48150-1793
(734)421-6600
LIVN #19

Searchlight
BOOKS

What
Are Earth's
Cycles?

# Investigating the

# Rock
# Cycle

Mary Lindeen

**Lerner Publications ◆ Minneapolis**

**Alfred Noble Library**
**32901 Plymouth Road**
**Livonia, MI 48150-1793**
**{734}421-6600**

3 9082 13140 5832

APR 1 0 2017

Copyright © 2016 by Lerner Publishing Group, Inc.

Content Consultant: Alan Boudreau, Professor of Earth and Ocean Sciences, Duke University

All rights reserved. International copyright secured. No part of this book may be reproduced, stored in a retrieval system, or transmitted in any form or by any means—electronic, mechanical, photocopying, recording, or otherwise—without the prior written permission of Lerner Publishing Group, Inc., except for the inclusion of brief quotations in an acknowledged review.

Lerner Publications Company
A division of Lerner Publishing Group, Inc.
241 First Avenue North
Minneapolis, MN 55401 USA

For reading levels and more information, look up this title at
www.lernerbooks.com.


**Library of Congress Cataloging-in-Publication Data**

Lindeen, Mary.
    Investigating the rock cycle / by Mary Lindeen.
      pages cm. — (Searchlight books. What are Earth's cycles?)
    Audience: 8–11.
    Audience: Grade 4 to 6.
    Includes bibliographical references and index.
    ISBN 978-1-4677-8058-2 (lb : alk. paper) — ISBN 978-1-4677-8337-8 (pb : alk. paper) — ISBN 978-1-4677-8338-5 (eb pdf)
    1. Rocks—Juvenile literature. 2. Geochemical cycles—Juvenile literature.
I. Title.
QE432.2.L565 2016
552'.06—dc23                             2015000954

Manufactured in the United States of America
1 – VP – 7/15/15

# Contents

# Chapter 1

# THE ROCK CYCLE

Rocks are everywhere on Earth. They are at the bottoms of lakes and oceans. They are in the soil. They are even in our streets. Where do all these rocks come from?

The Grand Canyon is a beautiful rock formation in Arizona. What are some other places where you might find rocks?

Most rocks are made of minerals.  Minerals are solid materials that do not come from plants or animals. Rocks are usually made up of more than one kind of mineral.

AMETHYST IS A MINERAL THAT IS OFTEN USED IN JEWELRY.

# THESE ROCKS IN SCOTLAND WERE FORMED MILLIONS OF YEARS AGO.

Rocks are constantly being created, destroyed, and created again.  This natural process is called the rock cycle.  It has been going on for billions of years.

Rocks are changed by weather, erosion, heat, and pressure. These forces destroy rocks. But the rocks do not go away. They just get broken apart or moved. Destroyed rocks will become new rocks in different places. Earth recycles its rocks!

Erosion is the gradual wearing away of a substance by wind, water, or ice. Erosion caused these arches to form over millions of years.

## Rocks Change

Rain and ice break rocks apart.  Chemicals weaken rocks.  Gravity pulls rocks down.  Rocks crack against other rocks.  Wind and water move pieces of rock.

Extreme heat changes rock.  Rock gets buried deep under Earth's surface.  Heat makes the rock soft.  It melts and mixes with gases.  New rock forms when the melted rock cools again.

Water can get into cracks in rocks.  When the water freezes, the ice expands.  Over time, this can cause rocks to break apart.

These rocks were pushed up from below Earth's surface.

Pressure inside Earth changes rocks. Pressure and heat together make rocks squish instead of break. The minerals in the rock get pressed together very tightly. This changes the minerals. The minerals get stretched and pulled. They flatten out. Pressure can also push rocks up. Rocks that were buried get moved to Earth's surface. Then erosion wears them down again.

# Types of Rocks

There are three main kinds of rocks. They are igneous, sedimentary, and metamorphic. Each kind is formed by the rock cycle. During this cycle, one kind of rock can change into another. But these changes do not happen quickly. Change can take millions of years.

## THE ROCK CYCLE

igneous rock

cooling

melting

erosion

magma

sediment

heat and pressure

erosion

melting

erosion

pressure and crystal formation

metamorphic rock

heat and pressure

sedimentary rock

# See the Cycle

The rock cycle creates three main categories of rock. But rocks can be categorized in other ways too. You can group them by shape or color, for example.

See if you can find ten different rocks outside. Look at them closely. Divide the rocks into groups. Make a label for each group. For instance, one group could be "Shiny Rocks" and another could be "Dull Rocks." Explain why you put each rock into its group.

# Chapter 2

# IGNEOUS ROCKS

Even on a cold day, Earth's inner layers are hot. They are hot enough to melt rock. This melted rock is called magma. Magma rises toward Earth's surface because of changing pressure inside the planet. Magma cools and hardens as it rises.

The red substance in this photo is melted rock. What will happen to this melted rock after it cools?

Hardened magma becomes igneous rock. Most magma cools and hardens belowground before it reaches the surface. This magma fills cracks in Earth's crust.

THIS ROCK FORMATION IN SPAIN IS MADE OF HARDENED MAGMA.

Igneous rock under Earth's surface can take thousands of years to harden. Crystals form over time. Crystals are clear or almost clear minerals. The crystals lock together as the rock forms. The rock is very hard and strong as a result.

DIORITE IS A HARD IGNEOUS ROCK WITH MANY CRYSTALS INSIDE.

Granite is one example of this kind of igneous rock. It has many large crystals. They give granite a speckled appearance. Granite can be polished until it is very smooth. It is also very hard. That makes granite ideal for buildings and statues.

This statue of Martin Luther King Jr. was carved from granite.

Granite forms deep underground. So how do people get to it? Tectonic plates make up Earth's crust. These plates slowly move and collide. This movement lifts some underground rock up to the surface. This process is known as uplift.

## TECTONIC UPLIFT

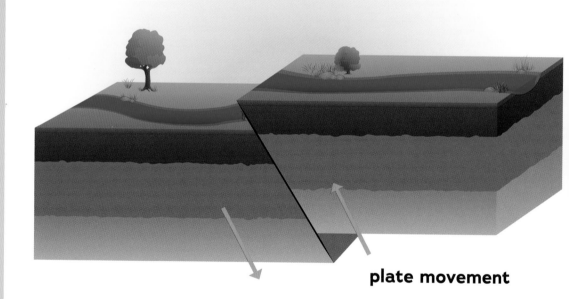

plate movement

# VOLCANO ERUPTION

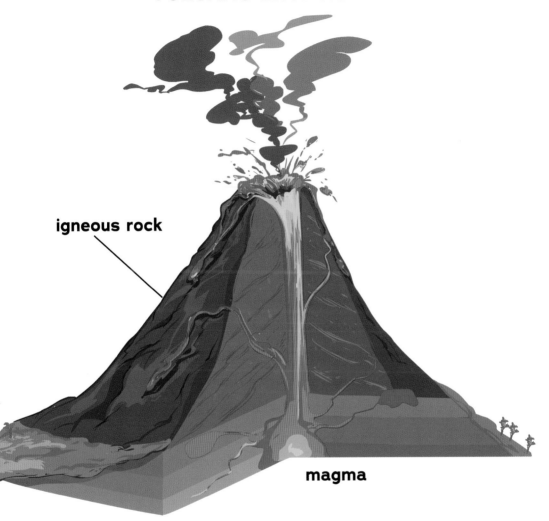

igneous rock

magma

Sometimes magma rises all the way up to Earth's surface. When this happens, the magma erupts from a volcano. Magma that erupts is called lava. Lava cools quickly. It also hardens and becomes igneous rock.

The most common type of lava forms a dark rock called basalt. This formation in Northern Ireland is known as the Giant's Causeway.

Basalt is the most common kind of rock in Earth's crust. It makes up most of the ocean floor. Railroad tracks are often built on top of basalt rocks. Crushed basalt is often used to make roads too.

Some lava cools so fast that it forms obsidian. This smooth igneous rock looks like shiny, black glass. Long ago, people used obsidian to make knives and arrowheads. In modern times, a doctor's scalpel might have an obsidian blade.

# See the Cycle

Pumice is another kind of igneous rock. It is full of holes. It is very rough and light. Get a pumice stone at a drugstore or a bath shop. Rub the pumice gently on your feet. What happens? Now fill a tub with water. Put the pumice stone in the water. What happens?

## Recycling Igneous Rock

We know magma is made of melted rock. But where does it come from? Both sedimentary and metamorphic rocks can be reheated deep underground. This makes new magma.

**Millions of years ago, these igneous rocks were magma underground. That magma came from other types of rocks.**

In millions of years, these igneous rocks will become other types of rocks.

And what happens to an igneous rock after it forms? It can erode to form sedimentary rock. Or it can be deeply buried to form metamorphic rock. These changes are all part of the endless rock cycle.

# Chapter 3

# SEDIMENTARY ROCKS

Sedimentary rock is formed from layers of sediment. Sediment is solid pieces of natural materials. Plants die and crumble. Animal bones decay. Shells break into pieces. All of these bits and pieces become sediment.

In time, these shells will break into pieces and become sediment. What are some other materials that can become sediment?

Sediment can also come from igneous rock. Over time, rain and glaciers break down the rock. Wind, rivers, and ocean waves carry away tiny pieces. These pieces become sediment.

Sediment can come from metamorphic rock too. Uplift brings metamorphic rock to Earth's surface. Then erosion wears the rock down. The rock breaks into smaller pieces. These pieces become sediment.

This glacier will break down rocks. Then the pieces of rock will become sediment.

Water and wind move sediment from one place to another. The sediment slowly collects in layers. Layers build up at the mouth of a river. They build up on the bottom of a lake. Sediment collects on the sea floor.

**A group of starfish rests on the sediment at the bottom of the ocean.**

## How Sediment Becomes Rock

Over thousands of years, sediment layers get pressed together. New layers pile on top of old layers. There is water between the grains of sediment. This water has chemicals in it. These chemicals can make crystals form. The crystals act like glue. They hold everything together.

THIS CLIFF HAS MANY VISIBLE LAYERS OF SEDIMENTARY ROCK.

THIS FISH DIED MANY YEARS AGO. BUT ITS REMAINS ARE PRESERVED IN A SEDIMENTARY ROCK.

We can see the layers in many sedimentary rocks. Scientists study the layers. Some layers have fossils of plants and animals that lived long ago. This helps scientists learn how the world has changed over time.

# Examples of Sedimentary Rocks

Have you ever made a sand castle? In a million years, that sand could become rock. The sand could build up in layers. Then the layers could harden into sandstone.

Many years from now, the sand on this beach could be part of a sedimentary rock.

Sandstone is a common sedimentary rock. It is made from tiny grains of rocks and minerals that have been pressed together. Sandstone is mostly made of a mineral called quartz. Sediment from other kinds of rocks is also found in sandstone. Sand near a river, in the desert, or on a beach can form sandstone.

These buildings on the European island of Malta are made with bricks cut from sandstone.

Many beautiful rock formations are made of limestone, such as this cave in Italy.

Limestone is another kind of sedimentary rock. It can form in shallow ocean waters. Most limestone is made of sediment from shells, coral, and other ocean life. Limestone has many uses. It is often crushed. Then it is used in concrete and in buildings. Limestone powder is used in paper and paint.

## Recycling Sedimentary Rock

Erosion is a big part of the rock cycle. It changes igneous and metamorphic rocks into sedimentary rock. Erosion can also turn old sedimentary rock into new sedimentary rock.

Sedimentary rock can also become igneous rock. But first, the sedimentary rock must change into metamorphic rock. This happens very slowly under Earth's surface.

**Mount Everest is the highest peak in the world. It is made of sedimentary rock. Fossils of ocean animals have been found near the top of the mountain.**

# See the Cycle

Find some sand, twigs, and small rocks. Put them in a clear bottle. Fill the bottle halfway with water. Put the lid on the bottle and shake it. Then wait until the sediment settles. Write down what you observe.

# Chapter 4

# METAMORPHIC ROCKS

Tectonic plates collide and create uplift. But uplift does not always bring rocks to the surface. Sometimes uplift buries rocks deeper underground. Higher temperatures make these rocks softer. And higher pressure squeezes these soft rocks into new shapes. Rocks formed this way are called metamorphic rocks.

Sometimes uplift brings rocks to Earth's surface, like the formation seen here. What else can uplift do?

## Features of Metamorphic Rock

Some metamorphic rock has stripes, or bands. Heat and pressure have rearranged the minerals. The minerals line up in layers. The layers make colored bands in the rock.

Not all metamorphic rock has bands. Sometimes heat and pressure do not make the minerals rearrange. Instead, they form large crystals.

Some metamorphic rocks, like this one, have bands that are straight. Others have bands that curve and bend.

Marble is a kind of metamorphic rock. It does not have bands. Before marble forms, it is limestone. The main mineral in limestone is calcite. When calcite heats up, it changes. The calcite grows bigger crystals. These crystals sparkle in a piece of broken marble.

Polished marble is smooth and shiny. People use marble for floor tiles. Marble can also be carved into sculptures.

Different colors of marble can be used to make beautiful patterns on floors.

# See the Cycle

Put several balls of cookie dough on a baking pan. Ask an adult to place the pan in an oven. Watch as the dough hardens and turns into cookies.

Scientists often call metamorphic rocks "cooked rock." This is because heat changes the rock. It is similar to how an oven's heat changes dough into cookies. Cookies will bake in about ten minutes. Metamorphic rock does not "cook" so quickly. It can take millions of years to form.

## Recycling Metamorphic Rock

Metamorphic rock changes too. Uplift can push it up to Earth's surface. Then erosion breaks it down into sediment. It can become sedimentary rock. Or it can become metamorphic rock again. It can also melt to become magma and then igneous rock. The rock cycle continues.

**Years and years of erosion created this amazing rock formation in Bolivia.**

# Science and the Rock Cycle

Get a candy bar that has layers of caramel and nougat. Ask an adult to cut the candy bar in half. The layers inside the candy bar are similar to the layers of sedimentary rock.

Put the candy bar into a resealable plastic bag and seal it tight. Press down on the bag until the candy bar is soft and flat. See how the heat and the pressure of your hands change the candy bar. This is similar to the way heat and pressure change sedimentary rock into metamorphic rock.

Take the flattened candy bar out of the bag. Put the candy bar into a microwave-safe bowl. Ask an adult to cook the chocolate bar in the microwave for one to two minutes. Let the melted chocolate cool and harden. Notice how the ingredients look different compared to how they looked when you first cut the candy bar in half. This is similar to the way heat changes metamorphic rock into igneous rock.

# Glossary

**crystal:** a clear or almost clear mineral that has many flat faces

**erosion:** the gradual wearing away of a substance by wind, water, or ice

**fossil:** the remains of an animal or a plant from millions of years ago that is preserved as rock

**gravity:** the force that pulls things toward Earth's surface

**igneous rock:** rock that is formed by magma, or molten rock

**magma:** melted rock found beneath Earth's surface

**metamorphic rock:** rock that is produced when extreme heat and pressure change one type of rock into another

**mineral:** a solid natural material that has a crystal structure

**rock cycle:** the process by which rocks are created, changed from one form to another, destroyed, and then formed again

**sediment:** solid pieces of material that are carried by water, wind, or ice from one place to another

**sedimentary rock:** rock that is formed by layers of sediment in the ground being pressed together

**tectonic plate:** a large section of Earth's crust that moves around because of the molten rock moving beneath it

**uplift:** the rising up of a part of Earth's surface as a result of tectonic plate collisions

**volcano:** a mountain that forms over an opening in Earth's crust through which lava, ash, and gases erupt

LERNER

SOURCE™

Expand learning beyond the printed book. Download free, complementary educational resources for this book from our website, www.lerneresource.com.

# Learn More about the Rock Cycle

**Books**

Lawrence, Ellen. *What Is the Rock Cycle?* New York: Bearport, 2015. This title combines colorful photographs and interesting facts to help readers understand the rock cycle.

Nelson, Maria. *The Rock Cycle*. New York: Gareth Stevens, 2014. In this book, Nelson explains all types of rock and how they are created.

Walker, Sally M. *Researching Rocks*. Minneapolis: Lerner Publications, 2013. This informative book explains how to research rocks and how rocks help us learn about Earth.

**Websites**

**The Geological Society: The Rock Cycle**
http://www.geolsoc.org.uk/ks3/gsl/education/resources/rockcycle.html
Visit this site to view an animated version of the rock cycle.

**Mineralogy4Kids: The Rock Cycle**
http://www.mineralogy4kids.org/rock-cycle
This useful website has charts to help you identify what type of rock you have.

**MIT Video: Rock Cycle**
http://video.mit.edu/watch/rock-cycle-13017
This page includes a lively video that explains the three types of rocks.

# Index

# Photo Acknowledgments

The images in this book are used with the permission of: © Martin M303/Shutterstock Images, p. 4; © J. Palys/Shutterstock Images, p. 5; © Ivan Kravtsov/Shutterstock Images, p. 6; © starmaro/ Shutterstock Images, p. 7; © Serg Zastavkin/Shutterstock Images, p. 8; © Darren J. Bradley/ Shutterstock Images, p. 9; © Baloncici/Shutterstock Images, p. 10 (bottom left); © Skynavin/ Shutterstock Images, p. 10 (bottom right); © Artography/Shutterstock Images, pp. 10 (top center), 21; © Budkov Denis/Shutterstock Images, p. 10 (top left); © Bozena Fulawka/Shutterstock Images, p. 10 (top right); © jaminwell/iStockphoto, p. 11; © RZ Design/Shutterstock Images, p. 12; © holbox/Shutterstock Images, p. 13; © Tyler Boyes/Shutterstock Images, p. 14 (left), 14 (right); © Julie Clopper/Shutterstock Images, p. 15; © daulon/Shutterstock Images, p. 16; © corbac40/ Shutterstock Images, p. 17; © Kanuman/Shutterstock Images, p. 18; © Rob Kemp/Shutterstock Images, p. 19; © tupatu76/Shutterstock Images, p. 20; © Anna Biancoloto/Shutterstock Images, p. 22; © Robert Cicchetti/Shutterstock Images, p. 23; © Vilainecrevette/Shutterstock Images, p. 24; © Leene/Shutterstock Images, p. 25; © Marcel Clemens/Shutterstock Images, p. 26; © Anna Abramskaya/Shutterstock Images, p. 27; © David Ionut/Shutterstock Images, p. 28; © AG-Photos/ Shutterstock Images, p. 29; © Pal Teravagimov/Shutterstock Images, p. 30; © AndersPhoto/ Shutterstock Images, p. 31 (top); © xpixel/Shutterstock Images, p. 31 (bottom); © thodonal88/ Shutterstock Images, p. 31 (center); © Thomas Barrat/Shutterstock Images, p. 32; © Siim Sepp/ Shutterstock Images, p. 33; © Vladyslav Danilin/Shutterstock Images, p. 34; © LightwaveMedia/ Shutterstock Images, p. 35; © Jess Kraft/Shutterstock Images, p. 36; © oksana2010/Shutterstock Images, p. 37.

Front cover: © iStockphoto.com/Beboy_ltd.

Main body text set in Adrianna Regular 14/20.
Typeface provided by Chank.